A
Preacher Girl's
Ride of Faith

*Life isn't about how many times you get
bucked off but whether or not you get back on.*

It's about the ride.

Barbie Brown Glunt

ISBN 978-1-7366825-0-0 (Paperback)
ISBN 978-1-7366825-1-7 (Digital)

Copyright © 2021 by Barbie Brown Glunt
All rights reserved. No part of this publication may be reproduced, distributed, or transmitted in any form or by any means, including photocopying, recording, or other electronic or mechanical methods without the prior written permission of the publisher. For permission requests, solicit the publisher via the address below.

Double Bar B Publishing Barbara A. Glunt
207 Hill Farm Road
Dunbar Pa 15431
barbaraann777@zoominternet.net

Printed in the United States of America

To my identical twin sister, Deborah
Jean Brown Rosensteel,
for her compassionate and loving spirit
and always seeing the best in people.
Your life was a living testimony
as well as your death.
I miss you so.
We will ride again.

To my mother,
Margaret Alexander Brown,
who endured the responsibilities of
raising a large family.
It was your unconditional love and patience
that kept us together.
Thanks for always being there,
I will always love you

To my younger sister,
Sherri Brown Miller,
I know you always felt you were in the
shadow of the twins.
But through your courage, quiet
demeanor, and meek disposition,
you came to the light and slayed the giants.
You are such a blessing to the family.

ACKNOWLEDGMENTS

With sincere appreciation, I would like thank my two dearest friends and sisters in the Lord who stood with me on my ride, Cynthia J. Brown LaPorte and Maryann L. Evans. We prayed through many situations and learned to slay giants with spiritual warfare. We held each other through the tears and trying times and celebrated as Jesus gave us the victories. Thank you both so much, I couldn't have endured without you.

I would like to thank Vaughn and Jackie McDiffett for all their encouragement and believing in me. Your kindness did not go unnoticed. Thank you for being a part of my life.

I would also like to thank Pastor George and Sonya McLean for mentoring me in the early years of my Christian walk. Know that your labor was not in vain. God bless you for your faithfulness.

I would also like to thank Pastor Roger and Patty Richter for all of your encouragement and being a part of the Barn of Praise Ministry. God Bless.

CONTENTS

Preface 9

1. Mistaken Identity: The Case of the Green Sweater ... 11
2. The Birthday Surprise 18
3. Star and the Blue Ribbon 22
4. Someone Was Watching 26
5. A Train Wreck to the Rescue 29
6. Growing Pains 34
7. No Greater Love 37
8. Crossing Over 40
9. Forged on the Farrier's Anvil 44
10. A Dried, Thirsty Land 50
11. Speaking Out My Faith 56
12. Raindrops from Heaven: The Miracles 62
13. Call of the Wild 72
14. Who Said You Can't Pray for Money? 76
15. Never Too Old to Get a Boyfriend 80
16. The Block Layer's Folly 83
17. Pickup of the Day 89
18. Mattie Comes Back to Life 93
19. The Lost Dogs 96
20. The Dream of Doves 101
21. Prayer of Salvation 104

PREFACE

Life isn't about how many times you get bucked off but whether or not you get back on. It's about the Ride.

The ride of life can be very unpredictable. You never know from one day to the next what will happen. Will you be happy and successful, or will you experience failures and sadness?

The only thing that is predictable is that God is right beside you on this ride. He is there encouraging you to be the best that you can be. He is involved with every situation and knows your every concern and need. You can trust and hand Him over the reins of your ride.

Let Him be in control and lead you in the right path. He has your best interests in mind. He will never leave or forsake you. He loves you with an everlasting love.

1

Mistaken Identity: The Case of the Green Sweater

Being an identical twin can be very precarious with many ups and downs. Thankfully, there are more ups than downs. At the tender age of six, though, I learned my first lesson of the consequences of having someone look exactly like me.

Debbie and I were in first grade at South Side Elementary in South Connellsville, Pennsylvania. Mom, being the proud mother she was, always dressed us the same; from the identical color hair ribbons to the patent, sleek black leather shoes, everything matched. Unbeknown to me, Debbie, upon entering the classroom one morning, decided she was going to erase the blackboard. After erasing it, she then proceeded to take off her green sweater and sat down in class. The next thing I knew, the teacher confronted and accused me of erasing the blackboard. I assured her that I would do no such thing and did not know who did. She insisted that I had to be the culprit because I had the green sweater on. Though I pleaded innocent, she paddled me in front of the class and grounded me during recess. All the kids went outside to play; and there I sat, humiliated, hurt, and wondering who had erased the blackboard.

After dismissal, Debbie and I were briskly walking home, with her keeping a pace about fifteen feet ahead of me, when she turned around and sheepishly admitted that she was the one who erased the blackboard. She took off running. I chased her the whole way home. When we flew into the house, I reported it all to Mom. Mom assured us that she would straighten the whole mess out. So, the next day, Mom sent us to school with a note for the teacher explaining the mix-up. Upon reading the note, being quite taken back she had made a mistake and not sure exactly how to rectify the situation, looked at both of us and announced that the next time I did something wrong, she would paddle Debbie. I looked at her in total disbelief—relieved that she knew the truth but a little confused on the due process of law. I was shamed and punished for something I didn't do, and Debbie gets off the hook!

Sometimes life takes us into situations where our identity is mistaken, and we are completely innocent but accused anyway. Or when our identity is stolen and used to rob us of our hard-earned possessions or blessings.

Consider the story of Jacob and Esau, twin sons of Isaac and Rebekah. Jacob pretends to be Esau before his aging father and gains the blessings of the firstborn, which we read in Genesis 27:1–17:

When Isaac was old and his eyes dim, he wanted to bless Esau his older son before his death. He asked Esau to go out to the field, hunt game and make his favorite food that his soul may bless him before he dies.

Rebekah heard what Isaac spoke to Esau. She immediately called Jacob her son and asked him to obey her voice and do whatever she commanded him. She told him to go out to the flock and bring her two choice kids of the goats, that she would prepare the savory food that Isaac loved. Then Jacob would take it to his Father, that he may eat it and bless him instead of Esau.

Jacob is concerned because his brother is a hairy man and he is smooth skinned. He is afraid that his Father will feel him and find out that he has been deceived, and bring on himself a curse instead of a blessing.

Rebekah puts Esau's smelly hunting clothes on him and wraps his hands and the back of his neck with the skins of the kid goats, so he would appear to be hairy like his brother.

Isaac questions him a few times and has some doubts but eventually blesses him. Here is the blessing he received as read in Genesis 27:27–29:

> And he came near and kissed him; and he smelled the smell of his clothing, and blessed him and said: "Surely, the smell of my son Is like the smell of a field Which the Lord has blessed. Therefore, may God give you Of the dew of heaven, Of the fatness of the earth, And plenty of grain and wine. Let peoples serve you,

> And nations bow down to you. Be master over your brethren, And let your mother's sons bow down to you. Cursed be everyone who curses you, And blessed be those who bless you!"

What a blessing! He would have the dew of heaven, the fatness of the earth, and the plenty of the grain and wine. Peoples would serve him and nations would bow down to him. He would be master over his brethren, and his siblings would bow down to him. So, Jacob gains the blessing of the firstborn by disguising himself as his twin brother Esau.

Now, let's read on what happens next in the story:

> "Now it happened, as soon as Isaac had finished blessing Jacob, and Jacob had scarcely gone out from the presence of Isaac his father, that Esau his brother came in from his hunting. He also had made savory food, and brought it to his father, and said to his father, "'Let my father arise and eat of his son's game, that your soul may bless me." And his father Isaac said to him, "Who are you?" So, he said, "I am your son, your firstborn, Esau."
>
> Then Isaac trembled exceedingly, and said, "Who? Where is the one who hunted game and brought it to me? I ate all of it before you came, and I have blessed him---and indeed he shall be blessed."

When Esau heard the words of his father, he cried with an exceedingly great and bitter cry, and said to his father, "Bless me---me also, O my father!"

But he said, "Your brother came with deceit and has taken away your blessing."

And Esau said, "Is he not rightly named Jacob? For he has supplanted me these two times. He took away my birthright, and now look, he has taken away my blessing!" And he said, "Have you not reserved a blessing for me?"

Then Isaac answered and said to Esau, "Indeed I have made him your master, and all his brethren I have given to him as servants; with grain and wine I have sustained him. What shall I do now for you, my son?"

And Esau said to his father, "Have you only one blessing, my father? Bless me---me also, O my father!" And Esau lifted up his voice and wept. Then Isaac his father answered and said to him:

"Behold, your dwelling shall be of the fatness of the earth, And of the dew of heaven from above. By your sword you shall live, and you shall serve your brother; and it shall come to pass, when you become restless, That you shall break his yoke from your neck." (Gen. 27:30–40, italics mine)

So, we see here, by mistaken identity, Jacob steals his twin brother's Esau blessings of the first born. The words that Isaac his father spoke cannot be changed or turned back.

The Lord wants us to take seriously the words that we speak. We can speak blessings or curses over our children. Our biblical patriarchs knew the importance of the words of their mouths.

Also, it is intriguing to see that throughout the Old Testament, you can find Jesus for Jesus would come from the line of Jacob as said in Matthew 1:1–16. And Jesus would be the Master over all the brethren which the peoples will serve and nations will bow down to. As said in Psalm 72:11, "Yes, all kings shall fall down before Him; All nations shall serve Him."

Debbie and Barbie

Debbie, friend Dee and Barbie

Debbie, Mr. Avery, Janitor and Barbie

2

The Birthday Surprise

As Debbie and I got a little older, all we could think about was horses. We dreamed horses; drew horses; played horses; and watched every horse show on television like *My Friend Flicka*, *The Roy Rogers Show*, *The Black Stallion Returns*, *Bonanza*, and all the John Wayne Westerns we could squeeze in during the day were our constant companions. We pestered Mom and Dad constantly for a horse. Well, lo and behold, on our twelfth birthday, Dad along with Mom, comes driving up the driveway with a pony sticking its head out the back of their Willys Jeep. Debbie and I were so excited, we didn't know which way to turn first. As we pushed each other through the front door, there, standing like a royal steed from heaven, was our first pony. "His name is Nipper," my Dad informed us. "I got him down the road from Red Kimmel for twenty-five dollars." Our eyes were as big as saucers. To us, he was a million-dollar prize, an answer to our prayers, a dream that finally came true.

After Dad saddled him, we scrambled to see who would get on first. We didn't know anything about horses except what we saw in the shows. As I bravely stepped into the stirrup and sat down, the pony unexpectedly pulled the reins so hard almost out of my hands, lowered his head down, and around and around we went! Then he laid down and tried to roll over on me. Hey! This wasn't in the movies! I barely escaped alive! So much for our first horse. After a few more close calls, Dad finally announced that he was donating the pony to Camp Christian, a retreat camp for children up in the mountains. I never could figure that one out. I heard later, during the same year that pony was donated, there was a lack of Christians in the area.

Isn't life like that? What you see isn't always what you get.

In 1 Samuel 16:1, the Bible says, "Now the Lord said to Samuel, "How long will you mourn for Saul, seeing I have rejected him from reigning over Israel? Fill your horn with oil, and go; I am sending you to Jesse the Bethlehemite. For I have provided Myself a king among his sons."

This continues on to 1 Samuel 16:6–13:

> So it was, when they came, that he looked at Eliab and said, "Surely the Lord's anointed is before Him!"
>
> But the Lord said to Samuel, *"Do not look at his appearance or at his physical stature, because I have refused him. For the Lord does not see as man sees; for man looks at the outward appearance, but the Lord looks at the heart."* [my italics]

So Jesse called Abinadab, and made him pass before Samuel. And he said, "Neither has the Lord chosen this one." Then Jesse made Shammah pass by. And he said, "Neither has the Lord chosen this one." Thus Jesse made seven of his sons pass before Samuel. And Samuel said to Jesse, "The Lord has not chosen these." And Samuel said to Jesse, "Are all the young men here?" Then he said, "There remains yet the youngest, and there he is, keeping the sheep."

And Samuel said to Jesse, "Send and bring him. For we will not sit down till he comes here." So he sent and brought him in. Now he was ruddy, with bright eyes, and good looking. And the Lord said, "Arise, anoint him; for this is the one!" Then Samuel took the horn of oil and anointed him in the midst of his brothers; and the Spirit of the Lord came upon David from that day forward. So Samuel arose and went to Ramah.

When you look at this story, what is the main difference between David and his brothers? It wasn't the fact that his brothers were older and had better physical appearance and stature; it was the fact that David was the one keeping the sheep. He was watching over them, moving them to the best pastures and looking out for their welfare. He was about his Father's business, doing the will of the Father.

Jesus said in Matthew 7:21-23, "Not everyone who says to Me, 'Lord, Lord,' shall enter the kingdom of heaven, but he who does the will of My Father in heaven. Many will say to Me in that day, 'Lord, Lord, have we not prophesied in Your name, cast out demons in Your name, and done many wonders in Your name?' And then I will declare to them, 'I never knew you; depart from Me, you who practice lawlessness!'

So, appearances can deceive us. Always pray and ask the Lord for His direction and wisdom concerning a person or situation. Only He knows a person's heart.

3

Star and the Blue Ribbon

We had a little more success with our second pony, Star. She was a paint and much larger than Nipper. She was very docile; anyone could ride her—and ride we did. We rode that pony day and night. With eight children at home, she was mighty busy. Our riding skills were beginning to improve, and I started looking for an opportunity to learn more.

I heard about a local horse show being held over the weekend two miles down the road. I never entered a horse show before but was confident to give it a try. We didn't have a trailer to haul her, so I figured if I left early enough, I could ride her there in less than an hour. We made it in plenty of time, and I signed up for the first class. The announcer called the class, and before I knew it, I was in my first horse show!

This class was the open pleasure class. The horses must walk, trot, and canter smoothly on cue with their right leg leading, going both directions in the ring. The rider must be in proper position, holding their seat with their legs in correct alignment with their shoulders and heels. Around and around the ring we went. To tell you the truth, I didn't know what I was doing. I remember my face was beet red from the heat and a little embarrassed knowing I didn't have the training like the other riders. All I did was follow the next guy.

The judge told us to bring the horses in and line them up. I sat; not expecting any good would come of my efforts, when much to my surprise my name and number were called out. We won first place and the blue ribbon!

Needless to say, from then on, horses were in my blood. I spent many an hour sitting up jumps, gates, barrels, and anything I could get my hands on. My free time involved brushing, feeding, and watering Star. Every weekend, I would clean and polish up my tack. Isn't it amazing how a little encouragement and positive reinforcement impacts our life. That blue ribbon proved to me that I could be successful. It gave me incentive to go on and increase my riding skills.

As the Bible says, "A man has joy by the answer of his mouth, And a word spoken in due season, how good it is!" (Prov. 15:23).

These lessons in life were not only teaching me that perseverance and hard work pays off but also to believe in myself. Later in life when I accepted Christ as my Lord and Savior, I realized He was with me at that horse show. He was there, encouraging me to be all that I could be. And I always remember what Philippians 4:13 says: "I can do all things through Christ who strengthens me."

Debbie and I joined the local 4-H horse club. It was through the 4-H program that we learned the more intricate scenarios in raising and training horses. It gave us a social connection to people who had the same interests that we had. Our lives were now centered on horses. I couldn't figure out how a person could even live—if they didn't own a horse.

Sometimes, we think that our efforts and words are of no effect. But we never realize what an impact our attitude, words, and actions can have on the next person. The same is true with winning the lost. The Lord said in Isaiah 55:11, "So shall My Word be that goes forth from My mouth; It shall not return to Me void, But it shall accomplish what I please, And it shall prosper in the thing for which I sent it," and in 1 Corinthians 15:58 Paul writes, "Therefore, my beloved brethren, be steadfast, immovable, always abounding in the work of the Lord, knowing that your labor is not in vain in the Lord."

God's Word is the most powerful word you can speak. When another person hears it, it does something to them. Perhaps, it changes an old attitude, belief, notion or thought. The Lord showed me many years ago, whenever I mention the name of Jesus to anyone, it is not forgotten and is recorded in heaven. Just think, every time we speak the name of Jesus or point someone to Jesus, we get rewarded. Not only do we get rewarded in heaven, but Jesus also rewards us on earth. What a grand time that will be when we are standing at those pearly gates and Jesus says, "Enter in, my good and faithful servant. Great is your reward in heaven." Never stop serving Him! It will be well worth it. What a great Savior we serve!

Debbie on Star

4

Someone Was Watching

After a few years, Debbie and I outgrew the ponies and were now thinking bigger—horses. Debbie got offered a good deal from our neighbor Charlie Brothers. He had a very young colt that just got injured in his stall. His back ankle got caught between the boards but was healing nicely. He was a fine-looking sorrel colt with a nice blaze down his face. Debbie was thrilled, bought him for seventy-five dollars, and named him Flame. In the meantime, I traded Star and twenty dollars for a bay colt that I named Charger.

The first dilemma we faced was the fact that both colts were stallions and would have to be gelded. Because money was scarce, we couldn't afford a vet, so Dad asked one of his friends who dealt with farm animals to do the castration. Everything seemed to be going fine until I noticed that Charger wouldn't quit bleeding. He bled most of the day. I knew something was wrong, and I talked Mom into calling a vet. Late in the evening, a vet from Waynesburg drove up and gave us the grim news that Charger was in critical condition. He needed a blood transfusion immediately. With no time to waste, for Charger was getting weaker by the minute, the vet did an emergency blood transfusion using Debbie's horse Flame.

After the vet left, Charger lay down and wouldn't get up. The prognosis didn't look good. I purposed in my heart that I wouldn't leave him. I opened a lounge chair, got a blanket, and spent the night next to him. Charger, though exhausted from the day's events, barely able to lift his head, listened attentively as I talked to him, encouraging him to hold on.

The night seemed endless as I drifted off to sleep. But sometime in the wee hours of the morning, I heard my Dad's voice, "Barbie, look! Charger is up and he is eating." There he was, standing on all four and eating grass. I was so relieved and couldn't believe it. He was standing and eating. Dad stood smiling, looking in awe. But what amazed me through the whole ordeal was, I had a sensation of someone watching, someone was there. I could just feel it. I was not alone. Someone was watching and directing the whole event.

I didn't know who that someone was then, but now I know. That someone was Jesus. He is in charge. John 1:1–5 says,

> "In the beginning was the Word, and the Word was with God, and the Word was God. He was in the beginning with God. All things were made through Him, and without Him nothing was made that was made. In Him was life, and the life was the light of men. And the light shines

in the darkness, and the darkness did not comprehend it."

And John 1:14 says, "And the Word became flesh and dwelt among us, and we beheld His glory, the glory as of the only begotten of the Father, full of grace and truth."

All things were made for Jesus, by Jesus, and through Jesus. We belong to Jesus. Everything you see belongs to Him. You are not your own. Jesus made you just for Him. He has a purpose and a plan just for you. He bought you with a price—His blood. He knows everything that is going on in your life. He knew everything that was going on the night Charger almost died. He was there.

Hebrews 13:5 says, "Let your conduct be without covetousness; and be content with such things as you have. For He Himself has said, "I will never leave you nor forsake you."

Barbie on Charger and Debbie on Flame

5

A Train Wreck to the Rescue

My Dad was a fun, loving guy. He always had a smile on his face and a story to tell. Everyone loved my dad. I remember how he always made people feel welcomed when they came to visit. No one could roll out the red carpet like he could. Many an evening he would sit Debbie and I on his lap and play his guitar for us. With six brothers and another sister, we were always biding for his time.

Dad was an engineer on the B&O Railroad for forty years. He loved the trains and everything to do with the railroad. Four of the boys followed in his footsteps and worked on the railroad also. One of our favorite dogs was found in a boxcar by my brother David and brought home. Dad named her Boxcar Willie. Though Mom wasn't much of an animal lover, she loved that dog.

Dad spent many a day away from home, so the demand of raising such a large family always fell on Mom's shoulders. She was the one who had to keep the clothes clean, pack the lunches, and get everyone off to school and on the right bus. I couldn't figure it out—with finances always tight and so many mouths to feed—how she always managed to put a good, hot meal on the table every evening. Until one night when it all made sense.

It was summer. Debbie and I were busy with the horses, but I was worried. We had run out of feed, and the horses were on their fifth day without feed. We kept them in a small pasture, but it wasn't large enough to sustain them for long. I knew Mom and Dad didn't have the extra money to buy any. I didn't know what to do, so I prayed. I remember lying on the top bunk in our bedroom, gazing at the stars and moon out the window. I said, "Lord, I don't know what to do. You blessed us with these horses, and now we can't afford to feed them. But I am asking you to make a way where there seems to be no way. Amen."

In the middle of the night, I was startled out of my sleep to hear all the commotion. Dad was getting the boys up to go with him. A train had derailed a few miles out of Connellsville and a load of grain had spilled on the tracks. Dad and the boys left and a few hours later brought home barrels of grain! We had so many barrels that Mom had to make room in the basement. I couldn't believe it. Barrels of grain! We fed the horses for a year.

Now, I knew how Mom always had a hot meal on the table. The Lord is the Provider—He knows our needs, and He hears our prayers.

In Genesis 22:2, The Lord instructs Abraham, Then He said, "Take now your son, your only son Isaac, whom you love, and go to the land of Moriah, and offer him there as a burnt offering on one of the mountains of which I shall tell you." As they approached the place in Genesis 22:7–14, this is what happened:

> But Isaac spoke to Abraham his father and said, "My Father!"
>
> And he said, "Here I am, my son."
>
> Then he said, "Look, the fire and the wood, but where is the lamb for a burnt offering?"
>
> And Abraham said, "My son, God will provide for Himself the lamb for a burnt offering." So the two of them went together.
>
> Then they came to the place of which God had told him. And Abraham built an altar there and placed the wood in order; and he bound Isaac his son and laid him on the altar, upon the wood. And Abraham stretched out his hand and took the knife to slay his son.
>
> But the Angel of the Lord called to him from heaven and said, "Abraham, Abraham!"
>
> So he said, "Here I am."
>
> And He said, "Do not lay your hand on the lad, or do anything to him; for now I know that you fear God, since you have not withheld your son, your only son, from Me."
>
> Then Abraham lifted his eyes and looked, and there behind him was a

ram caught in a thicket by its horns. So Abraham went and took the ram, and offered it up for a burnt offering instead of his son. And Abraham called the name of the place, *The-Lord-Will-Provide*; as it is said to this day, *"In the Mount of the Lord it shall be provided."* (Italics mine)

Don't ever give up. The Lord is the Provider. Look to Him for all provision. He will make a way where there seems to be no way. With no money to buy feed and no way for me to get any, He causes a train to wreck and spill it's load of grain. How awesome is that! He can do anything!

Younger sister Sherri holding Boxcar Willie

Dad on B&O Engine

6

Growing Pains

When Debbie and I entered Junior High West, the principal and fellow teachers decided it was best to separate us into different classes. They thought it would be beneficial for us since we were constantly together in grade school and also because they had a difficult time telling us apart. We agreed but wasn't too happy about it. Now, the only time we saw each other was in the hallways between classes. The most we could do was wave at each other. But over the course of time, we adjusted to the change and became a little more independent. We were both on the quiet side and a little shy around people.

We had a lot of fun in school and were teased continually. In tenth grade, one of my favorite teachers was Vaughn McDiffett. He was constantly teasing me. He knew I was from a large family and we lived out in the country. In front of the entire class, he would ask me if I had running water out where I lived and if our outhouse was working.

I could feel my face getting rosy red and hearing the kids laugh, but I was afraid to look around. I knew he was just clowning with me and took it with a grain of salt. As boldness welled up in me, I actually got a few punch lines back at him. It made the day a lot more pleasurable and helped me from being so shy. I think he did it just to see me blush. Later in life, he and his wife and I became close friends. I eventually worked for him at his grocery store.

Being an identical twin has its moments. I'll never forget when Debbie's boyfriend Dan put his arm around me and was about to kiss me when I stopped him in the nick of time. "Hey! I'm not Debbie," I shouted. Embarrassed from the mix-up, he apologized and went his way.

And then there was the time, on the last day of senior high school, we decided to play a little joke. Through three years of high school, Debbie took all secretarial classes and I took academic. So, we wondered how many teachers would know us apart if we traded classes. I went to all of her classes and got her report cards, and she went to all of my classes and got mine. Not one teacher knew the difference, but we sure had fun telling them at the end of the day.

Debbie got married to Danny in August 1973, and Butch and I got married in March 1974. We were both excited about entering this next phase of life. She and Danny moved into a house in the village of Trotter; Butch and I moved into a mobile home in Little Summit.

In the fall of 1976, Debbie proudly announced to the family that she was pregnant. She and Danny were so happy, but little did we know that this happiness would soon turn into tragedy.

Debbie and Danny

Barbie and Butch

7

No Greater Love

*J*esus said in John 15:13, "Greater love has no one than this, than to lay down one's life for his friends." What Jesus said here is so profound and mind-boggling. To think that He loves us so much that He would die a horrible death on a cross for us. He took our place. I don't know another person who would do that for me. There is no greater love then that.

When I preach on this subject, the Lord reminds me that every time one of His disciples take their time to visit a shut-in, go to a hospital, take food to a needy family, they are laying down their lives for another. So, we might not be physically dying for someone; but we are sacrificing our time, finances, gifts and talents to help another. This is the same as laying down one's life for our friends.

I usually use Debbie's Testimony in my sermon for this is what she did, and I would like to share it with you: Revelation 12:11 says, "And they overcame him by the blood of the Lamb and by the word of their testimony, and they did not love their lives to the death."

A few months into the pregnancy, Debbie started complaining about her back hurting. Heating pads and ointments didn't seem to help. The local doctors couldn't find anything wrong. Nothing seemed to alleviate the pain. Finally, Mom took her to a specialist, and he informed us that her lungs were filling up with fluid. It was a serious situation that needed immediate attention. They rushed her to a nearby hospital and did an emergency procedure to tap her lungs. The next day, we got the grim news that it was cancer. Here she was, twenty-three years of age, happily married, excited about her first pregnancy, and now finds out she has cancer. I'll never forget the moment when Mom broke the news to me. We just embraced with an agonizing sobbing and fell across the bed. We couldn't believe it. How could this be happening? We were totally shocked!

The family was devastated. Mom and Dad were desperate for answers. After seeing local doctors and specialists, they told us that Debbie's only chance was to abort the baby and start treatments immediately. The word *abortion* was not in Debbie's vocabulary. She flatly refused the idea to abort the baby. The doctors said they couldn't treat her then. At six months into the pregnancy, Debbie went into labor and was rushed to Allegheny General Hospital in Pittsburgh. She underwent an emergency C-section and delivered a four-pound baby boy, in critical condition, who was rushed to West Penn Hospital to be stabilized. The baby had every life-support tube connected to him that they could connect. Debbie and baby were both in serious condition. A priest was called in to give Debbie her last rights, and a preacher man came to pray for her. Mom and I were just bewildered by the whole ordeal. We had Debbie in one hospital and her baby in another. We didn't know which way to turn first.

Prayer requests went out all over the community. People we didn't know were calling, offering their help and prayers. Churches put them on their prayer chains. After one exhausting month, they both started to get stronger and finally came off the critical list. The following month, they came home.

Debbie started the dreaded chemotherapy treatments, and in between times of being sick and her hair falling out, she did have some enjoyable moments loving her new baby and experiencing motherhood. Mom and I helped as much as we could, but we could see she wasn't physically getting any better. I did notice something different about her, spiritually, though. She seemed more contented, and the fear was gone. Her face was also glowing, and she was actually happy. She bought me a wooden cross to hang on my wall. I could see this amazing joy over her face. Something happened to Debbie!

8

Crossing Over

Debbie tried the best she could to find some normalcy in her life. She would pack Dan's lunch in the morning, tend to the baby as best she could, and then rest. Mom and I would come down in the afternoon to help her with the house work and clothes. She bought a new wig that really looked cute on her, so I got my hair cut to match hers. That summer, we both attended our brother's wedding and had some special times together. Some days were better than others. She even surprised me one afternoon with a house visit. She was so proud of her baby boy.

Later that fall, Mom heard of a new treatment for cancer in the Bahamas. Dan agreed to take a chance and plans were made to fly Mom, Debbie, and the baby to the Bahamas. They were there about a month. Debbie wrote me a few letters and said she actually felt better, but before we knew it, the tide turned on us again. Debbie was flown home in critical condition and met with an ambulance that took her immediately to Allegheny General Hospital in Pittsburgh.

I stood by her bed while Mom wiped her forehead with a cool washcloth. I'll never forget her last words to me. She said, "Barbie, enjoy your life, go swimming, ride those horses, and have fun. It's over before you know it." Debbie slipped into a coma.

Dad was working late that night on the B&O Railroad when I got a call into him to come quickly; Debbie wasn't doing too good.

Dad never did like to drive, and when he would, he wouldn't go too far from home. Pittsburgh is an hour's drive north of us. And to this day, I still can't believe he drove to the hospital by himself in the middle of the night. The hand of the Lord had to be upon him.

I waited for him at the door. When I saw him coming, I noticed that he stopped and looked up in the sky. I ran to him, and as I approached, I said, "Dad, Debbie is dying, she's dying."

He acted like he didn't hear me and said, "Do you see that?

"What?" I asked.

"The three stars around the moon," he answered. "When I was driving down, I asked the Lord to give me a sign that Debbie would be all right, and there it is. I've never seen anything like it." There in the sky was the moon in crescent shape with three stars on the back side of it. We both gazed in awe.

We spent the night around her bedside. Debbie went to be with the Lord in the early morning hours. Most of the family was there. We hugged one another and sobbed. We couldn't believe Debbie was gone.

On the way home, I noticed the sun had come out after a long period of cloudy days, and I felt a peace and strength like none other. It might take me some time to get back on this ride. I hit the ground pretty hard, but Jesus was there to buffer the fall.

The funeral home was packed full of people. Everyone loved Debbie. She never had a bad word to say about anybody but always saw the best in a person. Her life was a testimony as much as her death.

I stood beside the casket, and a stranger came up and introduced himself as a pastor. He told me that he had a chance to talk to Debbie in the hospital after she had her baby and that she accepted Jesus into her heart when he prayed with her. No wonder she was all glowing when she got home. She found Jesus!

Romans 10:9–10 says,

> That if you will confess with your mouth the Lord Jesus and believe in your heart that God has raised Him from the dead, you will be saved. For with the heart one believes unto righteousness, and with the mouth confession is made unto salvation.

And Jesus said in Mark 1:15, "The time is fulfilled, and the kingdom of God is at hand. Repent and believe in the gospel."

The day of the burial, I stood beside the casket and placed a flower on it. I asked the Lord this question: "Why didn't you take me instead of her since she had the baby?" Immediately, He answered me in His still, small voice, "*Because I have work for you to do.*" Though I lost my best friend, my twin sister, my confidante, I knew somehow everything would work out. I would ride again.

Dad and Mom holding Debbie's son Danny

9

Forged on the Farrier's Anvil

During the next few years, Butch and I kept busy working and planning the house we were going to build. I worked for Anchor Hocking in the payroll department, and Butch continued to work for McKinney Drilling Company.

I sure did miss Debbie though. I especially missed our nightly phone calls to each other. To this day, I can still remember her phone number. Losing your twin puts a void in your spirit that you just can't put into words. I felt like part of me was missing. There was a hole, a gap that no one could fill.

We got the house built in 1979 and in the late 80s built the barn. The barn wasn't a typical barn—it was my dream barn. It was very large with eight stalls and a tack room. The foundation was built out of concrete blocks with a cement center aisle. The second story had T1-11 siding and double pane glass windows. It actually looked like a house.

I left Anchor Hocking after Debbie died and was now helping to manage a convenient grocery store and doing the bookkeeping. Butch was doing a lot of traveling for his company. He would be gone during the week and home on weekends. At this time, I thought my ride of life was going pretty smooth until I was thrown off again.

As a bronc rider hits the dust before the eight-second whistle blows, so it was for me. After twelve years of marriage, Butch left me. My world came to a crashing halt. We had just finished the barn, worked on the driveway, and did some landscaping. How could he just leave me and everything we had worked for? It didn't make any sense. I was devastated.

The night before he left, I was sleeping and had a vision. The Lord Jesus appeared to me in this vision. I knew it was a vision and not a dream because I felt a tremendous peace come over me. I saw Jesus with His arms outstretched to me. Though I didn't see Him speak verbally, these words came to me: "Barb, you are going to go through something, but I will be with you." As fast as He came to me, He went away. Immediately, I awoke and knew something tragic was going to happen. Butch left that day, and thus began my spiritual journey.

After a month of separation, with no hope on the horizon, I was slowly going into depression. I quit eating, did not go anywhere except to work, and did not care to talk to anyone. So I thought, *Okay, Lord, you got my attention. You're dealing with me. You want me to go to church?* Though I was raised in the Catholic Church, I didn't believe in all their teachings and traditions and had quit going long before. I knew in my heart that there was something more.

I looked in the daily paper and saw twenty churches advertising services. So, I said, "I would go to church, but I don't know which one you want me to go to." I closed the newspaper and went to bed instead.

In the morning, upon arriving at work, the cake decorator, Lonnie, said, "How's it going, Barb? You'll probably get real religious out of this."

I said, "Yeah, sure," and proceeded to walk into my office. A few hours later, a man came in to fix the plumbing on the dock. Someone told me he was a preacher man. I eyed him up as he stood on his ladder and said, "Are you a preacher?"

"Yep," he replied.

"Do you have a church?" I questioned.

"Yep," he answered. I studied him a little more and asked, "Do you ever help anyone with a problem?"

He came down off the ladder, looked me square in the eye, and said, "Why, do you have a problem?"

"Yes," I said, "My dog left me and my husband left. I think I got a problem."

He knew this would take some serious downtime and asked if he could talk to me in the office. As I nervously sat down, he asked me straight out, "Barb, are you saved? Do you know Jesus?"

I replied, "I believe in God. Does that count?"

He responded, "That counts, but did you ever ask Jesus to come into your heart?"

I told him that I didn't quite know what he was talking about. I believed in Jesus all my life, but I didn't know what this *saved* word meant. He then invited me to visit his Free Methodist Church on the other side of Uniontown that following Sunday. Before he left, he had a word of prayer with me. When he was done praying, this strong feeling of peace embraced me. I knew this must be the right track and the direction the Lord wanted me to go.

I was looking forward to visiting his church, but in the back of my mind, I keep pondering the question, *Why did I have to go to church when Butch was the one who left me? Why isn't he the one who should be going to church?*

Isn't that how most of us are? We never want the spotlight to shine on ourselves. It's a lot easier to look at other people's sins than our own. Sunday morning couldn't come quick enough. I knew the Lord was dealing with me, and I wanted to see what He wanted.

Pastor Dale gave a straight salvation message. He preached not only to believe that Jesus died for your sins but to confess him as your Lord and Savior, repent of sins, and receive Him into your heart for all have sinned and fallen short of the glory of God. There is none righteous—no, not one. Romans 10:9–10 says, "That if you confess with your mouth the Lord Jesus and believe in your heart that God had raised Him from the dead, you will be saved. For with the heart one believes unto righteousness, and with the mouth confession is made unto salvation," and Jesus said in Mark 1:15, "The time is fulfilled, and the kingdom of God is at hand. Repent, and believe in the gospel." I ran to the altar, sobbing, repeating the sinner's prayer. I needed help, and I knew God was the only one who could help me.

The next day, Pastor Dale came to my place of work and said, "Well, Barb, how do you feel, you're saved now?"

I responded, "No, I'm not."

He said, "What do you mean, you're not? Anyone who came to my altar like you has to be saved!"

I said, "No, I'm not because I know something has to happen in my spirit, and nothing happened."

Pastor Dale just shook his head and walked out in disbelief.

I must have been a real hardhead. It took the Holy Spirit three more days of drawing me, and then finally lying on my bed—with no preacher, no priest, no one—it just clicked! I cried, "Lord, you died for me, and I am so sorry. I really messed up my life. I'm not even worthy to be saved. Would you please forgive me?" I said it with every fiber in my being. I meant it from the bottom of my heart.

When I got real with the Lord, He got real with me. The glory of God filled my room. I felt the Lord wash me from the top of my head to the soles of my feet. Now, I knew I was saved. This was Jesus! I felt him embrace me as it says in Song of Solomon 2:6, "His left hand is under my head, and his right hand embraces me." Jesus was holding me. What a peace divine! I was saved! Halleluiah! John 3:3-7 says, "Jesus answered and said to him, 'Most assuredly, I say to you, unless one is born again, he cannot see the kingdom of God.'" Nicodemus said to Him, "How can a man be born when he is old? Can he enter a second time into his mother's womb and be born?" Jesus answered, "Most assuredly, I say to you, unless one is born of water and the Spirit, he cannot enter the kingdom of God. That which is born of the flesh is flesh, and that which is born of the Spirit is spirit. Do not marvel that I said to you, 'You must be born again.' The wind blows where it wishes, and you hear the sound of it, but cannot tell where it comes from and where it goes. So is everyone who is born of the Spirit."

When I got saved, Jesus's spirit witnessed in my spirit. It was no guessing act, I was truly saved. I was now born-again—saved on January 19, 1987.

Denise Smith, one of my best friends when we worked at Village Grocer, and Barbie

10

A Dried, Thirsty Land

I stayed at Pastor Dale's church for three months. He taught me about the love of Jesus and how to witness to people. The congregation was very caring and supportive. He was a great pastor and helped me tremendously, but I knew there was something more—something more the Lord wanted me to learn.

My cousin Donnie invited me to Calvary Assembly of God in South Connellsville, Pennsylvania. A new pastor, Pastor George McLean, had just taken over. When I entered the church, I could feel that special peace again and knew this was where the Lord wanted me.

I learned for the first time how to pray, how to read my Bible. I read how Jesus was baptized, by submersion, as a grown man before he started His ministry. Jesus led by example and showed us that baptism is meant to be an outward public commitment that you are going to follow Him. He says, "Repent and be baptized." You have to be old enough to repent and make that decision in your heart. Some churches baptize babies, and that's okay. But a baby can't repent and make a commitment to follow Jesus. Babies are saved whether they are baptized or not because they have not reached an age of accountability.

Mary took baby Jesus to the temple and dedicated Him to the Lord. So, by this example we should dedicate our children to the Lord and make the commitment that we, as parents, will do our best to raise them in the Lord. It is not a five-minute ritual act but a lifetime commitment to help them to follow Jesus.

I was ready to make that kind of public commitment. I had enough of following traditions of men and doctrines of churches. I wanted to follow a true leader.

Later that summer, the church had a baptismal service in a swimming pool in the mountains. I couldn't wait to go. Lining up with others with my baptismal robe on, my heart was beating with excitement as Pastor McLean gave the invitation. I stepped forward. He placed the cloth over my nose and gently submersed me in the cool water. It was "down with the old man and up with the new." A wonderful, heavenly, divine feeling came over me. Being obedient to the Lord's command to be baptize sure has its benefits, and I knew this was another step in the right direction.

I was like a dry, thirsty land—like a sponge that couldn't get enough of the Lord. I witnessed to many people and invited them to church. My countenance was glowing, and I was beaming with God's love. You know the old saying "You can lead a horse to water but can't make him drink"? I was led to the living waters and couldn't drink enough! It reminded me of the story in John 4 when the Samaritan woman meets the Messiah:

A woman of Samaria came to draw water. Jesus said to her, *"Give Me a drink."* For His disciples had gone away into the city to buy food.

Then the woman of Samaria said to Him, "How is it that You, being a Jew, ask a drink from me, a Samaritan woman?" For Jews have no dealings with Samaritans.

Jesus answered and said to her, *"If you knew the gift of God, and who it is who says to you, 'Give Me a drink,' you would have asked Him, and He would have given you living water."*

The woman said to Him, "Sir, You have nothing to draw with, and the well is deep. Where then do You get that living water? Are You greater than our father Jacob, who gave us the well, and drank from it himself, as well as his sons and his livestock?"

Jesus answered and said to her, *"Whoever drinks of this water will thirst again, but whoever drinks of the water that I shall give him will never thirst. But the water that I shall give him will become in him a fountain of water springing up into everlasting life."*

The woman said to Him, "Sir, give me this water, that I may not thirst, nor come here to draw."

> Jesus said to her, *"Go, call your husband, and come here."*
>
> The woman answered and said, "I have no husband."
>
> Jesus said to her, *"You have well said, 'I have no husband,' for you have had five husbands, and the one whom you now have is not your husband; in that you spoke truly."*
> (John 4:7–17, emphasis mine)

This Samaritan woman was trying to find true love, contentment, and happiness in her relationships; but all of them left her unfulfilled and empty. She went through five husbands, and the one whom she now had was not her husband. Think about how many people you know who go through one relationship after another and are never happy. This Samaritan woman is no different from us. She was looking for that security of peace, love, and happiness in a person.

Jesus saw her need. He saw her longing to be satisfied. He saw the hole in her spirit that no man could fill. He sits by a well and waits for her. She is that important to Him. He didn't wait to condemn her, but to point her to Himself. What she needs is Him!

I can relate with her. My whole world was based on my relationship with Butch. I was looking for the same things that this Samaritan woman was looking for and kept coming up short. What I needed was Jesus. Thank God, He took the time to come looking for me. He allowed me to be bucked off this ride of life so that He could help me get back on a bigger and better ride with Him holding the reins.

Some saints said, after seeing my zeal and exuberant spirit, that I was on my honeymoon with the Lord, and that I would get over it. Thank God, they were wrong. Never lose your first Love. Stay with Him. Stay focus on Him. Keep drinking the living waters. He will give you that peace, contentment and happiness that you are looking for. He's the best!

During this time of growth, the Lord spoke to me one night in prayer. Again, He asked me a question, "Barb, will you give up everything and follow Me?" I said, "Yes, I hate this life. I lost Debbie and now Butch. What do you want me to do?" He didn't answer me immediately but I knew in my heart as I kept following Him, His plans, in due time, would be revealed.

I continued serving the Lord, giving of my time, talent, and finances. I kept praying for Butch and for the Lord to heal our marriage. I'll never forget the day my eldest brother came to visit. He sat me down and said it was time for me to throw the towel in, that our marriage was over, and that Butch was never coming home. He told me that it was time for me to move on with my life with men who were like that. I stood up, grabbed my Bible, and said, "My Bible says, 'Is anything too hard for God?' and I'm not giving up! End of conversation!" He left a little bewildered. I determined in my heart that I would ride this bronc.

Barbie getting baptized by Pastor George McLean

11

Speaking Out My Faith

Butch was gone almost a year, and things started getting worse instead of better. I was losing my full-time job, finances were getting low, and I took a horse over to Scottdale to sell but couldn't make the sale. I drove back to the house, pondering my situation. I led the horse out of the trailer and walked her around the back of the house. It was a beautiful night—all the stars and moon were out and the heavens looked so serene. I stopped for a moment, looked up at the night sky, and spoke my faith. I said, "Lord, I've done everything you told me to do. I just want to remind you, Butch isn't home, I'm losing my full-time job, and I couldn't make a sale with this horse. But I am not giving up. I still got faith in You!"

As I walked closer to the barn, my name was called out. I heard, "Barb." I looked around and didn't see anyone so I continued to walk the horse into the barn. I put her into her stall and fed her.

Upon walking out of the barn, again, I heard, "Barb." I looked out over the corral area, but no one was there. It was only me and this horse, and the horse wasn't Mr. Ed. He couldn't speak. So, I said, "Lord, this must be you. I don't know what you want. I've been to every church service. I haven't missed a prayer meeting. I'm reading my Bible daily. I don't know what else you want me to do. So, I'm going into the house to take a shower and go to bed."

The next morning, Butch was home! The miracle happened! There he was, asking my forgiveness and if I would take him back. I looked at him in awe and total amazement. With the love of Jesus welling up in me, I accepted his apology, and we embraced like never before. He was gone almost a year. My prayers were answered!

Jesus said in Matthew 21:22, "And whatever things you ask in prayer, believing, you will receive." No matter how difficult the circumstances are or how gloomy the prognosis looks, hold on to your faith. Your faith is what the Lord is moved by. The Bible says in 1Peter1:6-9 "In this you greatly rejoice, though now for a little while, if need be, you have been grieved by various trials, that the genuineness of your faith, being much more precious than gold that perishes, though it is tested by fire, may be found to praise, honor and glory at the revelation of Jesus Christ, whom having not seen you love. Though now you do not see Him, yet believing, you rejoice with joy inexpressible and full of glory, receiving the end of your faith- the salvation of your souls."

There is something powerful about speaking out your faith. It becomes your sword in the Spirit.

David spoke out his faith when he went against Goliath:

> And the Philistine said to David, "Come to me, and I will give your flesh to the birds of the air and the beasts of the field!"
>
> Then David said to the Philistine, "You come to me with a sword, with a spear, and with a javelin. But I come to you in the name of the Lord of hosts, the God of the armies of Israel, whom you have defied.
>
> This day the Lord will deliver you into my hand, and I will strike you and take your head from you. And this day I will give the carcasses of the camp of the Philistines to the birds of the air and the wild beasts of the earth, that all the earth may know that there is a God in Israel.
>
> Then all this assembly shall know that the Lord does not save with sword and spear; for the battle is the Lord's, and He will give you into our hands."
>
> So it was, when the Philistine arose and came and drew near to meet David, that David hurried and ran toward the army to meet the Philistine.
>
> Then David put his hand in his bag and took out a stone; and he slung it and struck the Philistine in his forehead, so

> that the stone sank into his forehead, and he fell on his face to the earth.
>
> David prevailed over the Philistine with a sling and a stone, and struck the Philistine and killed him. But there was no sword in the hand of David. (1 Sam. 17:44–50)

The stone that David slung represents Jesus, God's word. In Luke 20:17–18, the Bible says,

> Then He looked at them and said, "What then is this that is written: 'The stone which the builders rejected Has become the chief corner stone'? Whoever falls on that stone will be broken; but on whomever it falls, it will grind him to powder." (Emphasis mine)
>
> It also says in Isaiah 28:16 Therefore thus says the Lord God: "Behold I lay in Zion a stone for a foundation, a tried stone, a precious cornerstone, a sure foundation; Whoever believes will not act hastily.

Slinging the stone represents putting our faith into action by speaking out God's word. We can have faith; but faith, without works, is dead. Speaking out your faith is mighty powerful in the spirit realm—it can slay giants, bring the dead to life, and bring home a lost loved one. Halleluiah!

Sometimes, this ride of life can get pretty rough, but we have the weapons to get the victory as the Word says in Ephesians 6:10–18:

> Finally, my brethren, be strong in the Lord and in the power of His might.
>
> Put on the whole armor of God, that you may be able to stand against the wiles of the devil.
>
> For we do not wrestle against flesh and blood, but against principalities, against powers, against the rulers of the darkness of this age, against spiritual hosts of wickedness in the heavenly places.
>
> Therefore take up the whole armor of God, that you may be able to withstand in the evil day, and having done all, to stand.
>
> Stand therefore, having girded your waist with truth, having put on the breastplate of righteousness, and having shod your feet with the preparation of the gospel of peace; above all, taking the shield of faith with which you will be able to quench all the fiery darts of the wicked one.
>
> And take the helmet of salvation, and the sword of the Spirit, which is the word of God; praying always with all prayer and supplication in the Spirit, being watchful to this end with all perseverance and supplication for all the saints—

One of the key scriptures in these verses, is 6:12 For we do not wrestle against flesh and blood, but against principalities, against powers, against the rulers of the darkness of this age, against spiritual hosts of wickedness in the heavenly places."

This scripture is so crucial to our daily existence. I really believe if we would lay this powerful scripture as a foundation in the lives of our children, our friends and families, all of our lives would be a lot happier, peaceful and productive. We would understand who the real enemy is, and by understanding learn how to engage the battle so Jesus can fight and win us the victories and blessings we desire.

The Bible says in 1Samuel 17:47: "Then all this assembly shall know that the Lord does not save with sword and spear; for the battle is the Lord's, and He will give you into our hands."

12

Raindrops from Heaven: The Miracles

Throughout God's Word, there is always the promises or blessings for being faithful, persevering through a trial and staying with the Lord. Job was blessed twice as much as he had before for enduring all his testings. Abraham was blessed after he was willing to offer Isaac up as a sacrifice to prove his love for the Lord. He would now be the father of many nations. Noah and his family was the only family saved from the flood that destroyed all humanity because he was found to be righteous. From his line, the whole earth would be repopulated. And the list goes on and on with Ruth, Rebecca, Jacob, David, King Solomon, etc.

Through every storm or testing of life, there are the miracles. Our God is the same yesterday, today, and forever. He is the same God today as He was in biblical times.

He changes not. So, the Word tells us to keep our faith in Him so we can be rewarded:

> Now faith is the substance of things hoped for, the evidence of things not seen. For by it the elders obtained a good testimony. By faith we understand that the worlds were framed by the word of God, so that the things which are seen were not made of things which are visible. (Heb. 11:1–3)

> But without faith, it is impossible to please Him, for he who comes to God must believe that He is, and that He is a rewarder of those who diligently seek Him. (Heb. 11:6)

My trial, though different in time periods and people, still had the same God; and two miracles were on the way.

After Butch came home, the Lord began healing our marriage. It wasn't accomplished in leaps and bounds but in small steps—a kind word, a reassuring hug, attentive discussions, etc. Now the Lord could work through me to show Butch His love. Now I could be the vessel to guide us in the right direction and path with His Word.

One Sunday morning, Pastor McLean announced an opening for children ministry and was looking for someone to take over the junior church. After looking around and seeing no one volunteered, I felt compelled to raise my hand and the hand of my cousin Cyndi. She hesitated and tried to stop me from raising our hands, saying, "You don't know what you are doing, we'll be stuck here for years." Needless to say, she didn't prevail, and we now became the directors of the junior church.

We began teaching fourteen children in the basement. I found two old puppets and threw a tablecloth over a table and thus began our puppet ministry. By the end of the next summer, the children ministry grew from fourteen to sixty-four children. We had to move out into the gym. What fun we had putting on skits, puppet shows, teaching God's Word, and ministering to the children needs.

One Sunday, I came home from church, went into my bedroom, shut the door, kneeled by my bed, and prayed. I said to the Lord, "Lord, you said in your word that if I was in your will, I could ask you anything. If I could make a difference in the life of a child, I would like to be given an opportunity. I ask in the name of your Son, Jesus. Amen."

Immediately, I felt raindrops fall on my head in my bedroom, not physically in this realm but spiritually in the spirit realm. They were hitting me on the top of my head. The only thing I knew about rain is that God sends it as a blessing. The Lord heard my prayer! Raindrops from heaven—wow! The blessing was on its way. I got up from the prayer and didn't tell anyone what I just prayed for. Over the next few weeks, the anticipation was overwhelming. What was God up to now? What kind of ride would this be?

About a month later, our neighbor, who was a single parent, was transported by ambulance to the local hospital with severe back pain. He was later transported to a Pittsburgh hospital where he died of heart complications.

His son, Eugene, who was six years old was left in the waiting room of the local hospital. I alerted Pastor McLean, and he and his wife went up and got the young child.

I couldn't sleep that night. I knew in my heart and in my spirit, that child was the answer to my prayer. He was supposed to be mine. After Pastor and his wife prayed about it, they agreed that the Lord wanted to bless our family with this new addition. So, I brought Genie home, whom we later named Jimmy since his birth father and another brother had the exact same name.

Jimmy was very excited about his new surroundings. His birth father was a very modest individual and very old-fashioned. He lived in a well-kept bungalow but had no indoor plumbing and cooked on a coal stove. He raised his own chickens and goats to eat. Every time I placed dinner on the table, regardless of what it was—it could be roast, steak, pork loin, or ham—Jimmy's eyes would get big as saucers, and he would say, "That looks like good chicken!" We would just chuckle and try to tell him the difference between the cuts of meats. We also could not get him out of the shower. He loved the water. Butch and I got the biggest kick out of his transition into the modern world. He put many a smile on our faces as we enjoyed watching his newfound discoveries.

Four years after we brought Jimmy home, I was still teaching the children in the local church. One Sunday, I taught about Hannah in the Bible who couldn't have children, so she went to Eli the priest and prayed for a child. She promised to raise the child in the Lord and give him back to the Lord, if her request was granted.:

> And she was in bitterness of soul, and prayed to the Lord and wept in anguish. Then she made a vow and said, *"O Lord of hosts, if You will indeed look on the affliction of Your maidservant and remember me, and not forget Your maidservant, but will give Your maidservant a male child, then I will give him to the Lord all the days of his life, and no razor shall come upon his head."*
> (1 Sam. 1:10–11, emphasis mine)

I never wanted to get pregnant after what happened to Debbie, seeing how we were identical twins. So, after I taught the children about Hannah, I went home, shut the door to my bedroom, got down on my knees, and prayed this prayer, "Lord, You did it for Hannah, You can do it for me. This time, I would like a baby boy. I want him to have brown hair, brown eyes, and be a happy baby. And if you give me a baby boy, I will raise him in your Word and give him back to You liked Hannah prayed." I could just see the Father telling Jesus, as He hands him a pen, "Did you get that, brown hair, brown eyes, and a happy baby?"

My faith was growing, and I learned to be more specific. I forgot to include the happy part with Jimmy; he would always curl my hair.

Immediately after the prayer, raindrops fell on my head again. The Lord heard the prayer! I could hardly believe it! Four years after praying for Jimmy, raindrops again fell on my head. I wondered what kind of surprise that would be. What would the Lord do?

I never told anyone about the prayer except Butch. I figured that I better prepare him ahead of time for I knew, without a doubt, this prayer would be answered also.

About a month later, our phone rang. A family we knew from the nearby county was on the line. The woman was agonizing over her circumstance that her daughter was pregnant—her husband had passed away a few years earlier, and she wouldn't be able to raise the child—asked if we would be interested. She was due in a few months.

Trying not to sound too excited, I said "Yes, we are interested."

For the next couple of months, I kept the situation in prayer before the Lord. I said, "Lord, if this is your will, let Butch lead in this situation." A lot of married couples could save themselves a lot of grief by learning to only go forward when both partners are in agreement.

On January 24, Butch and I were relaxing in the living room, when he questioned me, "Do you think she had the baby yet?"

"I don't know," I replied, "We could call."

On answering the phone, the birth grandmother announced, "My daughter had the baby today, we are giving him up tomorrow. Are you still interested?"

Are we interested? I've been waiting all my life for a baby! "Yes," I replied. I'll be right over."

Butch had previous plans already made, so he encouraged me to go ahead over and he would call to see what was happening. I picked up my cousin Cyndi, and we hurried over. Arriving at the hospital, my heart was racing. *What would he look like? What reception would we receive? How would the hospital handle this?*

I knew I had to just lay eyes on him. The elevator to the fifth floor seemed to take forever. As I stepped off the elevator and made a beeline toward the nursery, there he was—just as cute as cute could be. He had a little blue toboggan on his head, wide-eyed and looking around. I hugged the birth mother and grandmother and told them I would do my best to raise this child. I told them I would raise him in the Lord. We all cried together. It's never easy to give up someone you love. I know their hearts were breaking, but due to their circumstances, they thought it would be best for the child.

The hospital had to call an emergency meeting the next day. No one had ever done this before. I had no representative, no attorney, or agency; but I had all that I needed—I had the Lord!

The following day, I brought Joseph home from the hospital. Before I took him home, I stopped at the church and dedicated him back to the Lord on the altar. I named him Joseph William, William after my Dad's name.

It was snowing lightly as I entered the house. There he was in my arms all bundled up in his receiving blankets. I remember walking up the stairs to the living room in total disbelief. Admiring him, I said to the Lord, "Lord, you are awesome! Here he is, brown hair, brown eyes, and a happy baby." Joey is half American Indian. "You are awesome God! Thank You so much for our miracle." Butch greeted us with great excitement, as I announced, "Here he is, our son!" and laid him in his arms.

The next couple of days, the house buzzed with excitement. Relatives stopped over, and friends dropped by, blessing us with new blankets, bottles, and clothes for the baby. Everyone was excited for us, and Joey's arrival brought much happiness to our family. Jimmy was thrilled to have a baby brother. The greatest gift God could give us is a precious child, a new baby boy from heaven. How awesome!

"Behold, children are a heritage from the Lord,
The fruit of the womb is a reward.
Like arrows in the hand of a warrior,
So are the children of one's youth.
Happy is the man who has his quiver
Full of them; They shall not be ashamed,
But shall speak with their enemies in the gate." (Psalm 127:3-5)

Barbie, Jimmy and Butch

Barbie holding Joey

Joey and Jimmy washing up

Jimmy and Joey

13

Call of the Wild

When a person first gets saved and realize they are now redeemed, bought with the price of Jesus's blood, that they will never die but have eternal salvation, passed from death into life—it is such a wonderful enlightening experience. Everything looks brighter, clearer. Your whole perspective of life takes a 180-degree turn. You are now born again like Jesus says in John 3:3, "Most assuredly, I say to you, unless one is born again, he cannot see the kingdom of God." Some Christians say you are on your honeymoon with the Lord. Such was my case. It seemed like every prayer I prayed and every need or want I had, Jesus answered. All I had to do was ask, and the answer was on its way.

One night, after getting ready for bed, I decided I wasn't going to set my alarm clock. I asked Jesus to wake me up at 6:00 a.m. for work. I just thought I would wake up at that hour and be aroused or something.

It was a fall night, and I had my window up about six inches. I always liked the night air filling my room. I fell into a deep sleep, and before I knew it, the loudest hoot owl I ever heard hooted in my window. The noise actually scared me, and I jumped out of bed and raced to check the clock in the kitchen. Sure enough, it was 6:00 a.m.—right on the dot, not a minute late or early. I couldn't believe it! A hoot owl woke me at 6:00 a.m.! Was God proving himself to me, or what? I bet Jesus couldn't wait till 6:00 a.m. came to see my reaction! Isn't it great to know that the Lord, the great God of the universe, has a sense of humor?

Later in my Christian walk, I asked the Lord, "What was the conversation the day the hoot owl woke me up?" Here's the answer I got. Jesus and the Father were talking about how to wake me up.

Jesus said, "Well, Father, she doesn't live beside the ocean, so we can't send a ship. She doesn't live beside an airport, so we can't send a plane. She doesn't live beside the railroad tracks, so we can't send a train. What shall we send her?"

That's when the Father replied, "She lives beside the woods, I will command my hoot owl to wake her. I know she will talk about it, and it will increase her faith."

If you don't believe it happened, need I remind you how God worked through other animals in the Bible? Consider the story of Jonah:

> Now the word of the Lord came to Jonah the son of Amittai, saying, *"Arise, go to Nineveh, that great city, and cry out against it; for their wickedness has come up*

> *before Me* [emphasis mine]." But Jonah arose to flee to Tarshish from the presence of the Lord. He went down to Joppa, and found a ship going to Tarshish; so he paid the fare, and went down into it, to go with them to Tarshish from the presence of the Lord.
>
> But the Lord sent out a great wind on the sea, and there was a mighty tempest on the sea, so that the ship was about to be broken up. (Jon. 1:1–4)

> And he said to them, "Pick me up and throw me into the sea; then the sea will become calm for you. For I know that this great tempest is because of me." (Jon. 1:12)

> Now the Lord had prepared a great fish to swallow Jonah. And Jonah was in the belly of the fish three days and three nights. (Jon. 1:17)

Can you imagine that? The Lord commanded a great fish to swallow Jonah, and he was in its belly three days and three nights!

Or how about when Elijah prophesied in the days of the famine, did not God command ravens to fly over him and feed him, dropping bread and meat in the morning and bread and meat in the evening? Did not God command the animals to go two by two and seven by seven into Noah's ark to be saved from the flood waters? Did not God command Balaam's donkey to speak to him when he was going the wrong way?

The Lord Jesus is over all, including animals. He can command them to do His will anytime of the day or night. Nothing is too hard for Him!

14

Who Said You Can't Pray for Money?

*M*ost of us know how hard it is to make ends meet with utilities bills rising, unexpected medical bills, and day-to-day expenses piling up. Some days, we wonder if we will ever get through it all. It seems that no matter how hard we try, we always come up short. At least, I always thought that until the Lord showed me a better way.

Butch was always a hardworking construction man. Many a day he would drive for hours to get to his jobsite, sometimes fighting severe weather conditions and deplorable roads to make a living for our family. He would get up hours before his start time to make sure he was the first on the jobsite. His number 1 priority was to make sure the needs of our family was taken care of. He was a very good provider.

He started working as a teenager in a peach orchard down the road from his home place. From there, he got hired on pipelines throughout the state until he eventually got hired by McKinney Drilling Company in Delmont, Pennsylvania, as a laborer. McKinney Drilling is a foundation caisson company, which means they were the ones who drill the holes that supports the concrete piers and iron beams for many bridges, buildings, mines, and road jobs.

He had the hardest, dirtiest job. He would have to go down caisson holes, sometimes only thirty-six inches round and sixty to a hundred feet deep to jackhammer a bell in the bottom so it could be filled with concrete. It was very dangerous for sometimes the holes would cave in or fill with gases. Many a man lost their life doing this kind of work. Butch did it to the best of his ability, and oftentimes the company would send him out of state to finish a hole that no one else could do. He had the reputation for being the best in his field, and of course, the company wanted to keep him in that position. But as he got older, he was looking for an easier way to make a living.

He would often confide in me that he wanted to be an operator engineer with Local 66. Being an operator would be easier on him physically, plus it paid more money. He could run any piece of heavy equipment and was also an excellent mechanic. But he knew, with his learning disability in reading and writing, that his chances were few and far between; and he didn't think his company would ever give him an opportunity to advance.

One day after reading my Bible and studying how Elisha prayed in 2 Kings, I decided to put my faith into action. I noticed how Elisha would shut the door behind him, get alone with the Lord, and pray with all fervency.

Shutting the door behind him is significant for I believe it means shutting the world out—no cell phones, no computers, no tablets, nothing to interfere with my relationship with the Lord.

Psalm 91:1 says, "He who dwells in the secret place of the Most High Shall abide under the shadow of the Almighty." The secret place is the special time that you set aside for just you and the Lord. No one else. No one hears you, only the Lord. It's special, its sacred—just you and Him. Jesus said in Matthew 6:6, "But you, when you pray, go into your room, and when you have shut your door, pray to your Father who is in the secret place; and your Father who sees in secret will reward you openly."

I went into my bedroom, shut the door behind me, and prayed. I said, "Lord Jesus, you said, if I am in your will, I can ask you anything. You see how hard Butch is working, and I thank you for the money he is making, but we need more money. With insurance, taxes, utility bills, we are barely making it. You know Butch's heart, how he always wanted to be an operator engineer but never had an opportunity.

"I am sorry I didn't pray about this before, but in Luke 11:9–10, you said, 'So I say to you, ask, and it will be given to you; seek, and you will find; knock, and it will be opened to you. For everyone who asks receives, and he who seeks finds, and to him who knocks it will be opened.' So, I am asking in Jesus's name that you would make a way for him to get into the operator engineer's union, and I thank you for it. Amen."

Five days later, Butch called me from the shop and excitedly exclaimed, "Barb, you won't believe what happened. The business agent from the operator engineers just came in and signed me up! I am now an operator with Local 66!"

He went from making thirteen dollars an hour to twenty-three an hour. All it took was a five-minute prayer. Praise the Lord! What a great God we serve. If the Lord will do this for me, He will do it for you for the Bible says, "He is no respecter of persons" (Acts 10:34).

Butch with best friend Glenn Whitfield on construction site.

15

Never Too Old to Get a Boyfriend

One spring day, I had an unexpected visitor. My cousin Bertha came to the house. I knew something was up for in all of her eighty-one years, she had never stopped to see me. She lived by herself a couple of miles down the road in a whitewashed-looking frame house that her father built. She ran a grocery store from it and never had much of a social life. She never married and, as far as I knew, never had a boyfriend. I used to ride my bike or my horse to her store to cash in my pop bottles. Oh, how she would rant and rave when she saw the bottles. She hated cashing them in. The store was closed for quite a while before the visit.

She made some small talk and asked about the family and then got straight to the point. She looked square in my eyes and said, "You think you can pray so good? Then pray for me to get a boyfriend. All my life I wanted a boyfriend and never had one, so I want you to pray for me."

Quite surprised by the request, I mustered up all the faith I had at the time, with sweat beading up on my forehead, closed my eyes, grabbed her hands, and said, "Father, nothing is too hard for you. You hear this prayer and you see Bertha. You know her heart and how much she wants a boyfriend. She's looking to you. You said, if I am in your will, I can ask you anything in Jesus's name. So, in the name of Jesus could you please send Bertha a boyfriend. Amen." She looked satisfied, gather up her belongings, and left as abruptly as she came.

One month later, I heard through the grapevine that Bertha had a boyfriend! He owned a lot and camper at Big Bear Lake campgrounds. They spent many a day boating and fishing. I guess she was so busy with him, she forgot to come by and thank me for the prayer. Relatives keep me posted on her new lifestyle. He was her companion for the next ten years until she died. Just think, if she would have asked sixty years earlier, she could have had some grandkids!

In Luke 11:9–13, Jesus is speaking,

> "So I say to you, ask, and it will be given to you; seek, and you will find; knock, and it will be opened to you. For everyone who asks receives, and he who seeks finds, and to him who knocks it will be opened. If a son asks for bread from any father among you, will he give him a stone? Or if he asks for a fish, will he give him a serpent instead of a fish? Or if he asks for an egg, will he offer him a scorpion? If you then, being evil, know how

to give good gifts to your children, how much more will your heavenly Father give the Holy Spirit to those who ask Him!"

In John 14:12, the Word says,

> Most assuredly, I say to you, he who believes in Me, the works that I do he will do also, and greater works than these he will do, because I go to My Father. And whatever you ask in My name, that I will do, that the Father may be glorified in the Son. If you ask anything in My name, I will do it.

And also in John 15:7, Jesus says, "If you abide in Me, and My words abide in you, you will ask what you desire, and it shall be done for you."

16

The Block Layer's Folly

My faith was increasing as I saw the hand of the Lord in every situation we were facing. I was trusting Him more and more with my life. Jesus said in Matthew 6:31-34: "Therefore do not worry, saying, 'What shall we eat?' or 'What shall we drink?' or 'What shall we wear?' For after all these things the Gentiles seek. For your heavenly Father knows that you need all these things. But seek first the kingdom of God and His righteousness, and all these things shall be added to you. Therefore, do not worry about tomorrow, for tomorrow will worry about its own things. Sufficient for the day is its own trouble.

I was learning that when I would put the Lord first in my prayer life, finances, and relationships, he would add everything else that I needed. It was as simple as that: put the Lord first in your life and you will see how much easier this ride of life will be.

Butch was a mechanic, and his passion was working on and restoring old cars. Over the course of our married life, he restored '55 and '57 Chevys, a 1946 Ford Coupe, a Model A coupe, a 1955 Ford Pickup, and many others. And like most men, he always wanted his own dream garage, a garage big enough to work on and store his antique cars.

One day, as I was gazing out my bedroom window at a level area sixty feet from the house, I imagine how nice a big block garage would look there. I knew we didn't have the extra money for such a project and had no idea where we could get it, so I asked the Lord to help us financially to build the building.

A few weeks passed, nothing unusual happened. It seemed like that prayer hit a brick wall. Then a notice came in the mail that the electric company wanted a right of way through our property to set a couple of poles and were willing to pay us three thousand bucks. Three thousand dollars! What a revelation! I didn't know the Lord worked through electric companies! That would be enough to get started on laying the blocks for the garage. Isn't God good?

Butch started working on the garage in his spare time, and occasionally he would get some of his friends and family to help. It was a big undertaking, and it seemed that everyone in the family had their hand in the project.

One block layer—I'll call him Rob—agreed to help us out over the weekend. He was a very talented block layer and knew his trade well. He was a little on the quiet side, but I could tell something was bothering him. One day, when he was taking a lunch break, he began sharing with me that he was having trouble with his relationship with his daughter. Apparently, his daughter had moved out and was into drinking and partying and doing things her father didn't approve of. He was very bitter with her and had such odds against her that they hadn't talked in months. He then proceeded to tell me, "If I saw her walking down the side of the road, I wouldn't give her the time of day and would walk on the other side!"

I tried to reason with him and told him how kingdom living is all about relationships and forgiveness is the key. The Bible tells us that we all have sinned and fallen short of the glory of God, that there is no righteous—no, not even one. I told him that the best thing he could do to heal their relationship was to humble himself and speak to her.

I was startled by his answer, as he proudly said, "I'll not humble myself to anyone!"

I stepped back from him and looked him in the eyes and said, "Oh yes, but you will humble yourself one of these days. You will humble yourself! For the Bible says that every knee will bow and every tongue will confess that Jesus Christ is Lord to the glory of God the Father." He went back to work quite agitated and said no more to me. A week later, after some unexplained bizarre events, he died at his house. Sad to say, we did finish the garage, but this young man did not live to see it.

How careful we need to be with the words of our mouths. Jesus says in Matthew 12:36–37, "But I say to you that for every idle word men may speak, they will give account of it in the day of judgment. For by your words you will be justified, and by your words you will be condemned." Always remember—God hears everything!

Relationships are so important, and having them in the right order is even more crucial. The first four commandments in the Ten Commandments is about our relationship with God in keeping Him first in our lives:

1. Have no other God before Me.
2. Make no graven image to bow down before it.
3. Do not take the Name of the Lord in vain.
4. Remember the Sabbath to keep it holy.

And the other six commandments are about our relationship with other people. Jesus, when he counsels the rich young ruler in Matthew 19:16–22 after he asks how he may have eternal life, tells him to keep the commandments:

> Now behold, one came and said to Him, "Good Teacher, what good thing shall I do that I may have eternal life?" So He said to him, "Why do you call Me good? No one is good but One, that is God. But if you want to enter into life, keep the commandments." He said to Him, "Which ones?" Jesus said, "'You shall not murder,' 'You shall not commit adultery,' 'You shall not steal,' 'You shall not bear false witness,' 'Honor your father and your mother,' and, 'You shall love your neighbor as yourself.'" The young man said to Him, "All these things I have kept from my youth. What do I still lack?" Jesus said to him, "If you want to be perfect, go, sell what you have and give to the poor, and you will have treasure in heaven; and come, follow Me." But when the young

man heard that saying, he went away sorrowful, for he had great possessions.

Jesus only quoted the last six commandments for the rich young ruler had broken the first four commandments for he had his riches before the Lord.

It says in Matthew 22:35–40, a lawyer challenged Jesus:

> Then one of them, a lawyer, asked Him a question, testing Him, and saying, "Teacher, which is the great commandment in the law?" Jesus said to Him, "'You shall love the Lord your God with all your heart, with all your soul, and with all your mind.' This is the first and great commandment. And the second is like it: 'You shall love your neighbor as yourself.' On these two commandments hang all the Law and the Prophets."

Blocks for new garage

17

Pickup of the Day

I bought a beautiful registered black Quarter horse mare named Sanzi in the early '80s. She was a very good riding horse, and I entered her into some local shows around home. I mostly did Western pleasure classes with her. Later, I bred her to a big chestnut stallion with flaxen mane and tail named High Ball Bars.

I always dreamed of having a beautiful golden palomino with a white mane and tail like Trigger, the one Roy Rogers had. Little did I know that the Lord knows our hearts desires and dreams. He says in Psalm 37:4, "Delight yourself also in the Lord, And He shall give you the desires of your heart." Unbeknown to me, when you breed a black horse to a chestnut horse, your chances of getting a palomino was very high.

In April of 1983, Sanzi, my all-black mare gave birth to a palomino colt with a white mane and tail. I was ecstatic—my very own palomino colt with a white blaze down his face! I couldn't believe it. Could a girl get any more blessed than that?

Blaze grew into a very handsome colt. He stood sixteen and a half hands high with a golden coat that glimmered in the sunrays. He was my pride and joy. He was quite a handful to ride, though, very headstrong, powerful, and unpredictable. He definitely was not for the novice. In fact, no one would ride him except me. Raising him from a colt, though, I got on to his tricky moves, stubbornness, and spoiled attitude. He generally would behave pretty well unless something out of the ordinary would scare him.

One day, I took him out for a ride on the waterline tract a few hundred yards from my parent's home. The waterline right of way stretched for a good eighth of a mile with a creek on one side and the township shed at the end. This was the best place that I could really give him his head and let him run.

As I let loose the reins and gave Blaze his head, he took off as fast as he could. His powerful legs dug in for all it was worth with the wind beating against my face, and literally taking my breath away, we were off. All went well for the first few moments, and then I saw it—a bright, freshly painted blue pipe sticking up on my far left. I thought, *This isn't going to go over very well.*

As soon as Blaze saw the pipe, he started bucking. He bucked so hard that I flew off, high into the heavenlies. I actually had time to think how much this was going to hurt when I landed, especially with a pile of gravel beneath me. Later, when I would testify in churches about this incident, I told them that I was so high, the birds were waving at me!

As I hit the gravel pile, the air was knocked out of me, and I couldn't speak. I was face down in the gravel with only enough strength to raise one arm to motion for help. Again, in my despair, I cried out to the Lord—in my thoughts this time, since I couldn't breathe—and said, "Lord! Please send someone to help me!" All at once, I heard the sound of a big truck stopping. I heard the brakes squeaking and the motor coming to a halt. I thought, *Thank you Lord, for sending someone to help me. Thank You! Could it be the Salvation Army, the Red Cross, or maybe the army corps of engineers?*

The man's voice was shaking as he asked, "Madam, are you OK?"

"Yes," I squeaked out as he gently pulled me to my feet. I could see through blurred vision that it wasn't the Red Cross, Salvation Army, or the army corps of engineers. It was the garbageman, making his rounds! I was the pickup of the day! Thank God for garbagemen. He proceeded to help me catch Blaze, and I cautiously limped passed my parents' house on Blaze's far side so they couldn't see me. A garbageman to the rescue, who would of ever imagine?

The Lord speaking in Psalm 91:14–16 says,

> Because he has set his love upon Me, therefore I will deliver him; I will set him on high, because he has known My name. He shall call upon Me, and I will answer him: I will be with him in trouble; I will deliver him and honor him. With long life I will satisfy him, and show him My salvation.

Blaze and his mother Sanzi

Barbie on Blaze

18

Mattie Comes Back to Life

Horses are not the only animals in my life; I also love dogs. I heard many times growing up that I took after my paternal grandmother, Skip Brown. Rumor had it she used to ride horseback across the countryside and delivered babies. She was one of the few midwives in the area that did house calls. She also was an animal lover so I guess her love for animals was passed down to me.

One of my favorite dog shows on television was Lassie. To have a dog like that would be a dream come true. I had a couple of collies growing up and always envisioned myself doing something with dogs. It wasn't until after I got married, through the encouragement of one of my cousins, that I started raising and breeding boxers. I found the boxer to be a very personable dog, always ready to please and play. They also make a good watchdog too. My love for the breed grew, and at one point I had four females and one male. You probably heard the old cliché, "More isn't always better." I found this to be true the hard way. Because the more female dogs you have, the more likely they would get jealous of each other and fight.

One day, I heard a loud commotion outside by the dog kennel. I ran out to see what all the barking was about and found one of my older boxers literally swinging Mattie, a younger female, in circles by her throat. I tried yelling at them to no avail and had to grabbed a shovel to tried to separate them.

Joey, who was about ten years old at this time, came out and looked in disbelief. Mattie's body went limp mid-air before the other dog would let go. I ran to her and saw her eyes protruding, her tongue hanging out, and her body was motionless. As I stood over her, I said, "Joe, Mattie is dead, she's dead!"

The next thing I heard was this groaning bellow from the depths of his heart, as Joey cried out, "Oh God! Bring Mattie back to life!" Immediately, that dog came back to life and jumped up. I've never seen anything like it. Talk about the faith of a child—and not only faith but speaking out your faith with such fervency and conviction that the dead would rise! I often wondered if that was similar to how Jesus sounded when he groaned in His spirit and shouted, "Lazarus, come forth!" in John 11:43.

Joe had faith to believe that God could raise Mattie up, and by speaking out his faith, he put his faith into action. Remember what the Bible says: "Thus also faith by itself, if it does not have works, is dead" (James 2:17).

Reading the very first chapter of the Bible in Genesis, you will find that nothing happened in this realm until God spoke into the darkness:

A PREACHER GIRL'S RIDE OF FAITH

In the beginning God created the heavens and the earth. The earth was without form, and void; and darkness was on the face of the deep. And the Spirit of God was hovering over the face of the waters. Then God said, "Let there be light"; and there was light. (Gen. 1:1–3)

And the same thing happens as God calls forth the Heavens, the Earth, the Seas, the grass, the herb, the stars, the moon, the sun, living sea creatures, the birds, the cattle, and man.

And nothing is going to change in your realm until you begin to speak into your darkness. There is power in your words, why? Because the same Spirit of the Living God, lives in us!

Joey playing with boxer pupps

19

The Lost Dogs

Every summer, Bonnie and her husband Tom — would host their church's annual picnic at their house. They had a large outside pool and pavilion that would accommodate a large gathering. That year was no different as they were busy with all the preparations to make the day special. Tables and chairs were brought in, hamburgers and hotdogs were sizzling on the grill, and people were beginning to arrive.

Unbeknown to them, someone leaves the front gate open, and their two hound dogs Freeway and Chester takes off. After a few hours, the discovery was made that the dogs were missing. Everyone went into high alert and began scanning the nearby yards, fields, and roads.

Bonnie is becoming more and more frantic as time passes and there is no sign of the dogs. Her dogs are just like her children, and she loves them very much. Anyone who has lost a pet knows how heart-wrenching that can be. The entire congregation is looking for hours, but there is no sighting or trace of the dogs. The search continues for three days. Bonnie and Tom had called the nearby neighbors, placed posters up, and exhausted every avenue they could think of—and still no luck.

I was sitting at my dining room table doing some bookwork and never felt compelled to join the search, when Butch said to me, "Aren't you going to help Bonnie and Tom find those dogs?"

"Yes," I replied, "I'm going to help them." He proceeded going out the front door. I bowed my head and prayed, "Lord, you know where those dogs are. Would you please tell me? Thank you. Amen." Immediately, a thought came to me—*Call West Leisenring Post Office.*

West Leisenring is a small rural mining village about five miles south of us. It had a population of a few hundred people with a small post office alongside a road off the main freeway.

I hurried and grabbed the phone and dialed the number. A women's voice answered. I said, "I don't quite know how to ask you this, but we are looking for two hound dogs. One is black and white, and the other is brown and white."

She replied, "Honey, they just went by the door."

I was astonished to say the least. I flew out the front door and called out to Butch, "Butch, I found the dogs, the Lord just told me! I found them! I told you I was going to help them."

Joey jumped into the bed of the truck, and we sped up the road. Driving up and down the side roads by the post office, Joey, like the fine Indian trapper he was, called out, "Mom, there they are, under that truck!"

I stopped the truck, and Joe pulled them out. They were both exhausted and dehydrated, but they were alive! Praise the Lord! We delivered them into the arms of Bonnie with tears streaming down her face, totally ecstatic. She just couldn't believe they were home. I told her, "Isn't the Lord Good? He is our refuge in time of trouble." If only we would trust Him more.

After Elijah trusted in the Lord and executed all the false prophets in the Mt. Carmel victory in 1 Kings 18, he hears a threat from Jezebel and runs for his life. Why did Elijah run when he just showed the miraculous power of the Lord coming down as fire from heaven that consumed the sacrifice? Because he took his eyes off the Lord and had them on himself—his own abilities.

The Lord finds him hiding in a cave wanting to die, and spoke to him and said, "What are you doing here, Elijah?" After Elijah gives his meager reasons, the Lord says in 1 Kings 19:11–12,

> "Go out, and stand on the mountain before the Lord." And behold, the Lord passed by, and a great and strong wind tore into the mountains and broke the rocks in pieces before the Lord, but the Lord was not in the wind; and after the wind an earthquake; and after the earthquake a fire, but the Lord was not in the fire; and after the fire a *still small voice.*

That same still, small voice that Elijah heard is the same still, small voice that I heard and told me to call West

Leisenring Post Office. Why did I hear it? Because I prayed and asked the Lord to tell me, and then I listened. We could save ourselves so much time and anguish if only we would seek the Lord's face and spend time with Him. It's only when we take our eyes off Him and lose our focus that we find ourselves in a dark place.

Barbie on Blaze in parade lifting up Jesus

Pastor Barb preaching behind pulpit in The Barn of Praise

20

The Dream of Doves

The Lord speaks to us through His word and throughout His Word (the Bible). He speaks in various ways. Sometimes, He uses a prophet man or woman. Sometimes He uses dreams and visions. Sometimes He speaks audibly and sometimes He speaks in that still, small voice. Sometimes He will speak through events or signs like earthquakes, floods, births, deaths, miracles, rainbows, and many other examples. But the point is—the Lord speaks to us. He is the same yesterday, today, and forever; so it should be no surprise that He uses these varied ways today. Read what it says in the Bible:

> In the beginning was the Word, and the Word was with God, and the Word was God. He was in the beginning with God. All things were made through Him, and without Him nothing was made that was made. In Him was life, and the life

was the light of men. And the light shines in the darkness, and the darkness did not comprehend it. (John 1:1–5)

And the Word became flesh and dwelt among us, and we beheld His glory, the glory as of the only begotten of the Father, full of grace and truth. (John 1:14)

For the word of God is living and powerful, and sharper than any two-edged sword piercing even to the division of soul and spirit, and of joints and marrow, and is a discerner of the thoughts and intents of the heart. (Hebrews 4:12)

One night, I had a dream. In the dream, I was standing over by my barn, in the corral area. I was looking toward the house when all at once, I saw a dove flying around the front corner of my house. It was flying straight at me. But the strangest thing about this was, the dove had another dove riding on its back, piggybacking! I saw four wings flapping headed straight at me, and they smacked me in the center of my forehead and I fell backwards.

I immediately woke up and lay there, thinking, *What was that?* The Holy Spirit answered and said, "Double anointing to preach my Word!" I thought, *Wow! Double anointing to preach His Word! What an honor, what a calling!*

Then I argue with the Lord and reminded Him that I was a girl. He said He was well aware of that. Again, I said, "But I'm a woman." He again replied that He knew. He reminded me of His word in Galatians 3:26:

> For you are all sons of God through faith in Christ Jesus. For as many of you as were baptized into Christ have put on Christ. There is neither Jew nor Greek, there is neither slave nor free, there is neither male nor female, for you are all one in Christ Jesus. And if you are Christ's, then you are Abraham's seed, and heirs according to the promise.

He also reminded me that the first evangelist with the full gospel message: 'That not only did Jesus die for our sins, but that He arose again on the third day,' was a woman. Her name was Mary Magdalene. So the Lord does call women, and they are very vital and important for spreading the good news.

And so began the next phase of my spiritual journey. Sometimes we think that our lives are not important and how we can make a difference in someone's life. The truth of the matter is that everyone is important and everyone can make a difference. It's up to each one of us to lay down our lives, pick up our cross, and carry it. Follow Jesus! The Lord has work for each of us to do, and what a *ride* it can be!

21

Prayer of Salvation

The reasons I wrote this book and shared my personal true life experiences were to increase your faith, that the Lord Jesus can do anything; encourage you to draw closer to Him and know that He loves you with an everlasting love; to trust Him with your biggest problem and your smallest concern; to help you visualize that he is right beside you amid your everyday trials and tribulations; to know that you are never alone as He said, "I will never leave you or forsake you" (Heb. 13:5); and to bring you to a saving knowledge of the Lord Jesus Christ.

If it is your desire to know that you are saved, that you will live forever in Heaven with the Lord, that you will never die, and that your sins are forgiven; then repeat this prayer out loud. The only condition is that you mean it from your heart.

Dear Father,

I believe that Jesus Christ died for my sins, and arose again on the third day. I'm sorry for my sins and ask you to forgive me and wash me clean. Come into my heart and be Lord of my life. Thank you, Jesus, for saving me.

Once you give your heart to the Lord,

- start reading the Bible,
- keep up your prayer life,
- find a good Spirit-filled church that preaches the Word of God, and
- obey Jesus's command to be baptized.

ABOUT THE AUTHOR

𝐁arbie Brown was born in Connellsville, Pennsylvania, to Bill and Margaret Alexander Brown. She is one of nine children, which included six brothers and two sisters with one of the sisters being her identical twin, Debbie.

At the age of six, she and her family moved to a seven-acre farm in Dunbar Township in rural southwestern Pennsylvania, where her love for horses was able to blossom. It was through this love and responsibility of caring for them that she discovered her calling and the true love of the Lord Jesus Christ.

She married her husband Butch in spring 1974 and later adopted two sons, Jimmy and Joey. She graduated from California University of Pennsylvania with a bachelor's degree in education and took Bible courses from Berean Bible College.

She got her credentials from The Independent Assemblies of God and now pastors a church in the top of her barn called The Barn of Praise Ministry.

Come along with her as she learns to trust Jesus through many trials and adventures on her *ride of life*.

Contact Information

Pastor Barbara A. Glunt
The Barn of Praise Ministry
207 Hill Farm Road,
Dunbar, Pa, 15431
Contact nos.: 724-626-8186, 724-205-4152
Email me at Barbaraann777@zoominternet.net

www.ingramcontent.com/pod-product-compliance
Lightning Source LLC
Chambersburg PA
CBHW030912080526
44589CB00010B/272